LINES FOR ALL OCCASIONS

Flattery
& Faint Praise

Created and published by Knock Knock
Distributed by Who's There Inc.
Venice, CA 90291
knockknockstuff.com

© 2014 Who's There Inc.
All rights reserved
Knock Knock is a trademark of Who's There Inc.
Made in China

No part of this product may be used or reproduced in any manner whatsoever without prior written permission from the publisher, except in the case of brief quotations embodied in critical articles and reviews. For information, address Knock Knock.

This book is a work of humor meant solely for entertainment purposes. Actually utilizing the lines contained herein may be illegal or lead to bodily injury. The publisher and anyone associated with the production of this book do not advocate breaking the law. In no event will Knock Knock be liable to any reader for any damages, including direct, indirect, incidental, special, consequential, or punitive arising out of or in connection with the use of the lines contained in this book. So there.

Every reasonable attempt has been made to identify owners of copyright. Errors or omissions will be corrected in subsequent editions.

Where specific company, product, and brand names are cited, copyright and trademarks associated with these names are property of their respective owners.

ISBN: 978-160106585-8
UPC: 825703-50116-2

10 9 8 7 6 5 4 3 2 1

Contents

Introduction 5
Preparing to praise

Appearance 11
When beauty is as beauty does

Skills 27
When they are gifted

Personality 45
When they are who they are

Private Life 61
When home is where the heart is

Public Life 79
When you're out and about

Famous Flattery 95
When notoriety is noticed

"You should wear makeup more often."

Introduction
PREPARING TO PRAISE

Flattery—aka brownnosing, ass-kissing, or sucking up—has gotten a bad rap. In truth, puffery is an essential dialect in human communication, and those who consider themselves too "honest" to kiss butt do so at their own peril. As Niccolò Machiavelli and Dale Carnegie could attest, thoughtful ingratiation is a far more effective form of persuasion than intimidation. "More people are flattered into virtue than bullied out of vice," said nineteenth-century English writer Robert Smith Surtees, and his words are as true today as ever. Flattery is also crucial for moving ahead in life, particularly in the workplace. "A person who has every advantage to get ahead, except flattery, will sooner or later compete with someone else who has flattery, too," writes author Willis Goth Regier in his book *In Praise of Flattery*. "Intelligence, good looks, natural charm, and loyalty can be outmaneuvered by a charming intelligent flatterer." Or, as social satirist Lewis Lapham puts it, flattery aimed at bosses, much like suntan lotion or furniture polish, "cannot be too often or too recklessly applied."

But flattery is not necessarily phony. The most effective flattery bears some relation to the truth, however optimistically skewed. Indeed, if performed correctly, skillful buttering-up can be a positive, soul-enriching experience for both butterer and butteree.

Interestingly, it's not necessary for the recipient of praise to believe in its sincerity. In *You're Too Kind: A Brief History of Flattery*, Richard Stengel opines, "When it works properly, flattery makes the subject of the flattery a little happier and it makes the *flatterer* a little happier. And that is true even when the *flatteree* is wise to the flatterer."

Social science has borne this out in recent years. A 2010 study by the Hong Kong University of Science and Technology ("Insincere Flattery Actually Works: A Dual

Attitudes Perspective") found that people are subconsciously swayed by sweet talk, even when they know they are being manipulated. As reported in *Scientific American*, "the study's authors speculated that the susceptibility to flattery stemmed from [people's] simple desire to feel good about themselves . . . We may dismiss it offhand when a subordinate compliments our new haircut, but deep down we're thinking, 'You know what? I do look good.'"

The lesson? Whatever one's motives, carefully placing a kernel of truth in a compliment will mitigate any appearance of phoniness.

Of course, if your motives are truly dubious, you can harness the power of flattery to your own nefarious ends. The other side of flattery, faint praise (also known as the backhanded compliment), is a powerful tool. Sometimes an unalloyed kudo is neither a realistic reaction nor a smart tactic. With the backhanded compliment you maintain the upper hand. At the same time, you'll experience the added benefit of baffling the recipient—who is left trying to reconcile the words you've just said with the beneficent manner in which they were delivered. You will find within these pages numerous examples of such manipulation, along with many other verbal tidbits covering the length of the kindness-cruelty spectrum.

So go forth and soft-soap in good health, and without guilt. Know that quality flattery results in a win-win for both parties, and evil flattery—well, it's merely delicious.

APPEARANCE

When beauty is as beauty does

ON THE SUCK-UP SPECTRUM, appearance-related compliments are by far the easiest to give, and can offer the greatest immediate payoff. Besides small children, all people have physical insecurities, and everyone enjoys being noticed for some external attribute, however obscure. This includes the very beautiful, who can be surprisingly uncertain beneath their enviable exteriors.

Tip: The Seven Words

There's no faster way to turn a compliment into a backhanded jab than with the following seven words: "I don't care what everyone else says . . . " Preface any positive comment in this book with these words and you immediately spin it 180 degrees. The possibilities are endless—you can even think of ways to switch it up, like, "I think you're hotter than your sister, *no matter what I've heard from others.*"

Physical compliments are versatile tools for dealing with those inevitable individuals—coworkers, in-laws, etc.—whom we disdain, or with whom we share no personal affinity or interests, but whose good graces we require. Fortunately, it's easy to be honest when delivering such flattery, since a creative flatterer can always find *something* worthy of notice. A little goes a long way, though, especially if delivered with convincing sincerity and a dash of envy.

Beware: physical compliments are personal, and can quickly become too-familiar, especially at work or in public. When chatting up an attractive woman, for example, better to compliment her jewelry—or even her handbag—than her figure. The message will be received, and you won't sound like a lech.

On the other hand, if you are looking to unsettle a rival or take the pompous down a notch or two, backhanded physical compliments are also highly effective, and may be found abundantly in this chapter as well.

Age

If I were a bouncer, I'd totally card you.

I bet there isn't much you haven't seen.

I hope I look as good as
you when I'm old.

You're the best thing about
the last century.

Do you have cataracts or have
your eyes always sparkled?

You don't smell like an old person.

By the looks of you, I can
tell you're an old soul.

You make me dread going gray less.

APPEARANCE

Are you an AARP catalog model?

Your laugh lines really draw attention to your beautiful eyes.

You're bringing sexy back—way, way back.

Beauty

Didn't I see you coming out of the ocean once on a giant seashell?

If anyone could turn me gay, it's you.

You'd even be hot in the dark.

If beauty were time, you'd be eternity.

I could sell tickets to stare into your eyes.

You have a face
Vermeer would love.

———•———

You look so pretty—today!

———•———

The ancient Romans would
be jealous of that nose.

———•———

You look really nice in this light.

———•———

I almost didn't recognize you
today. You look so different.

———•———

You have a head for business
and a face for radio.

———•———

Your profile picture looks
nothing like you!

———•———

You're as pretty as a picture—
I believe it's called *The Scream*.

APPEARANCE

You should wear makeup more often.

———•———

Your smile makes the *Mona Lisa* look cranky.

———•———

You've got a smile so warm, it's contributing to climate change.

———•———

Your smile's so sweet, your dentist must have diabetes.

Stranger Things

Sometimes complimenting strangers really pays off. A Rutgers University acting student earned local recognition when he started posting inspirational quotes around campus as part of his RU Post-it Anonymous project. In a similar vein, the You Are Beautiful project in Chicago began by giving away thousands of tiny, silver, eponymous stickers. Within a decade, the project has grown into a business marketing "You Are Beautiful" around the globe.

Body

You look like the "After" photo.

With a body like that, you don't have to be smart.

You're the one person who doesn't look ridiculous in a Speedo.

I thought only porn stars looked like you.

Is your name Adonis?

Big muscles don't look dumb on you.

I'm jealous you don't have to wear a bra every day.

You have the body of an overworked food critic.

APPEARANCE

Pirates would fight over that booty of yours.

You look amazing from behind.

With a chest like that, who needs a life vest?

If you were taller, you could be a model.

You must have an amazing plastic surgeon.

You're as dainty as a drag queen.

Your wife must be an extraordinary cook.

You carry your weight well.

I admire you for resisting society's obsession with body shape.

Hot or Not?

Amateur lotharios might not know that poet Alexander Pope coined the phrase "Damn with faint praise," but they have long used the "neg," or backhanded compliment, in their arsenal of techniques. Popularized, and allegedly coined, by infamous pickup artist Mystery, the neg is a lighthearted negative comment used to lower a woman's self-esteem and open up conversation, especially if she's thought to be "hot."

Hair

I've got to get your stylist's number.

Well, at least you have good hair.

Bald is the new black.

I don't usually like brunettes, but it works for you!

APPEARANCE

I bet your secret to healthy
hair is never washing it.

Your comb-over
looks so natural.

You make me realize
that everyone should have
hair the color of their
favorite ice-cream flavor.

You're proof the mullet
never went out of style.

If Marge Simpson could rock
that hairstyle, so can you.

Your new 'do is so youthful—
like a twelve year old's.

You must be living with a hairdresser
because yours always looks great.

That facial hair must really
keep you warm.

Communist dictators would be
jealous of your mustache.

Grooming

You could be a shampoo model.

Do you bathe in happiness?

You don't sweat, you glow.

You smell as ripe
as a summer fruit.

Your bathing habits remind
me of my trip to France.

You don't sweat
much for a fat guy.

APPEARANCE

You smell like a hard worker.

That body hair works on you.

Nothing speaks to the resilience
of hair quite like your back.

You're one lady who deserves
a quick trip to Brazil.

Style

You're too well dressed to be straight.

Not everyone can make a
muumuu look sexy.

You don't mind if I copy
everything you wear, do you?

You're the first hipster I've met
who doesn't annoy me.

Now I see that tattoos can
actually be classy.

That's a lovely dress.
My grandmother was
buried in one just like it.

Great outfit. Black is
so slimming.

You manage not to look like
a hussy in those stilettos.

I love your collection of
ironic '80s T-shirts.

You always look new, even
when you're old.

Your stylish clothes
perfectly camouflage
your personality.

APPEARANCE

I love how you've matched your underwear with your T-shirt.

You wear enough bling to read by.

I love your free spirit! You just wear whatever you want, and you don't care what anybody thinks!

Hey, Baby!

Fed up with what she felt was constant harassment from men, Brooklyn artist Tatyana Fazlalizadeh began putting up posters around her neighborhood that asserted: "Women are not seeking your validation," and "My name is not baby, shorty, sexy, sweetie, honey, pretty, boo, sweetheart, ma." She called her 2012 project "Stop Telling Women to Smile." So boys, next time, try a nice smile and a nonthreatening "Hi."

SKILLS
When they are gifted

MOST PEOPLE ARE PROUDEST OF those accomplishments that they have worked hardest to hone. Therefore, feel free to praise other people's efforts and achievement abundantly, and rest assured your words will not fall on deaf ears.

Keep this in mind while toasting others' successes. Hard work should be acknowledged, especially

Smart Guys Finish Last

Even the brains at MIT's Media Lab can learn something new. At their 2013 SXSW conference party, guests received wristbands with "clever" compliments like "That's a nice dress. It would look great on my floor." The wristbands were the venue's idea, not something the MIT staff had hatched. Still, it led to Twitter outrage and a quick apology. The lesson: Check everything given out in your name. Also, there's a fine line between flattery and a sexist pickup line.

---

if you mention the recipient made a difficult thing look easy, and look good. Provide specificity by commending precise skills with breathless detail. And if you can be the first brave soul to publicly commend a person's new book, song, or painting, etc.—before the crowd follows suit—you will have a grateful ally for life.

If, however, you find little worthy of praise in someone's work or talents, don't despair. You can, without abandoning all sincerity, reach for flexible, vague adjectives such as "original," "unexpected," and "interesting." The insecure recipient will happily read what he likes into such terms, to everyone's mutual relief. You can skim these lines to find the *mot juste* that stealthily communicates your true opinion while just toeing the line of propriety.

At the same time, don't forget that some tone-deaf flatterees might be so sure of their skills that a backhanded compliment comes off sounding, to them at least, honestly laudatory. Win-win!

Mental Prowess

Your mind is like a steel trap.

If you were a dinosaur,
you'd be a thesaurus.

So, when are you due back
at the think tank?

You make me feel so brilliant.

You'd be bored to death
at a Mensa meeting.

Does Stephen Hawking know
he's got competition?

I can't believe they let you on
airplanes with that sharp intellect.

You're *street* smart!

SKILLS

The median age of Nobel Prize winners is 53.7—you have plenty of time!

Do you ever meet anyone as brilliant as you are?

You're so smart, computers stay awake worrying about *you*.

You're a tortured genius— emphasis on tortured.

I love how you just make everyone around you sound more intelligent.

You truly have a way with words— especially simple, easy-to-read ones.

I'd love to pick that brain of yours. It's like a thick scab.

Average isn't a bad thing.

You should get glasses. They'd
make you look so intellectual.

Congratulations on your graduation. It's
a miracle you finally finished something.

Financial Acumen

Cream always rises to the top.

Clearly you're from old money—
I had no idea you were so wealthy.

I usually hate rich people.

Is that a big wad of hundreds in your
pocket or are you just happy to see me?

You're not broke—you're bohemian!

There's absolutely no shame in
living with your parents.

SKILLS

What a cute little car.
I should downsize, too.

Your house is so cozy—
it'd be perfect for a hobbit!

You make poverty seem romantic.

Nobody can tell that's a knockoff.

It's All Greek to Me

The Greeks had a word for the antidote to flattery: *parrhesia*. Though it started out meaning "free speech," it eventually came to refer to boldness in telling someone what they didn't really want to hear—but needed to. Greek philosopher Diogenes said he thought that parrhesia was the most beautiful thing in the world, noting, "Other dogs bite their enemies. I bite my friends so that I may save them."

It must be so nice to be able to vacuum the whole house without having to change outlets!

Sometimes I wish I'd followed your path and chosen a career I loved over making lots and lots of money.

Physical Fitness

You make all the other marathoners look like 5K-ers.

How do you *do* that?

Did you ever play professionally?

I bet you played with barbells as a child.

You make me want to practice harder.

You're that wily veteran every team needs.

SKILLS

You're built for distance, not speed.

Wow, you sure scored a lot of touchdowns for a guy with your physique.

When you Zumba, your back fat bounces in perfect rhythm.

You sweat like a real athlete.

You're going for that classic underdog story, right?

Have you ever considered a career in sumo wrestling?

I see those yoga pants work for people who don't actually do yoga.

Your greatest athletic skill is not being a sore loser.

All Hail the Cabbie

New York City's informational 311 service has logged quite a few calls and emails praising the city's taxi drivers. According to the *New York Times*, the cabbies' good deeds included helping a woman after a mugging, returning an engagement ring, and enduring a yowling cat. But the jury's still out on whether a comment about a cab's signs "reminding us to cover our mouths when we cough" was flattery—or faint praise.

Your enthusiasm for trying is exceeded only by your record of failure.

———

Thanks for providing the warmest bench in the league.

———

At least you're not the *worst* one on the team!

———

You're a winner at losing.

Geek Smarts

What's it like being so out in front you're practically in the future?

How lucky for you that super-geeks are cool now.

I'm impressed by your artificial intelligence.

Didn't I see you at the midnight show of *Star Trek XXI*?

You're the coolest Dungeon Master I know.

I can see you know your way around a 20-sided die.

You have more talent in your thumb than you have in the rest of your body.

You have a great virtual personality.

You're a lot cuter than your avatar.

I bet your Comic-Con booth gets mobbed.

You have so many online friends—have you met any of them?

With that many followers, can I safely call you a twit?

You must be really well known on anonymous bulletin boards.

With access to the Internet, intelligence is less and less important.

Thanks for fixing my computer without belittling me once.

Artistic Talents

You're so gifted you should be wearing a bow.

You've got the skills to pay the bills and still have change left over.

You're so talented you could have your own variety show.

Did a team of angels descend from the heavens and teach you to sing?

With that voice, they could hear you in the balcony—and at the theater down the street.

You took that song and really made it your own.

Didn't you used to be famous?

I have VHS tapes of all
your best movies.

———•———

You were probably too
talented for the part.

———•———

Your art really makes a statement.

———•———

You are so . . . avant-garde!

———•———

Your painting looks amazing
from far away.

———•———

Well, art really *is* subjective.

———•———

Performance art is such an act of courage.

———•———

You dance better than all the
other middle-aged white guys.

———•———

Your pictures are worth 2,000 words.

SKILLS

Shakespeare called. He wants his genius back.

The Pulitzer committee won't know what hit them.

Your iambic pentameter is so intuitive.

Your novel is so good it should end with "BEGIN AGAIN."

Tip: Gesture Wisely

As the world gets smaller, hand gestures are becoming more universally understood—but don't count on it. You may think that complimentary thumbs-up is saying "yes, I like it!" but in Iran, Iraq, or Sardinia it will be read as "screw you!" In 1992, the first President Bush flashed the peace "V" to Australian bystanders with his palm inwards. Seems his advance team forgot to tell him it means "up yours" Down Under, and in England, too.

Congratulations on becoming a
contributor to a blog on the Internet!

You look amazing in
your author photo.

You write well enough
to self-publish.

There's a lot to like about your
writing, especially the periods.

Your creativity is rivaled
only by your grammar.

This is the best first draft
I've ever read.

Domestic Accomplishments

Your house is so clean. Did
you hire a housekeeper?

SKILLS

I've never seen such artfully
arranged clutter.

Even if I were on a diet I'd
eat your cheesecake.

Your brisket brings all the
boys to the temple.

This is almost as good
as my mother's.

You make a perfect
overcooked steak.

That tasted better than it looked.

I love your desserts. They've really
been helping me to avoid sweets.

Your food is so fresh and nutritious
that it doesn't need to taste good.

PERSONALITY

When they are who they are

FLATTERING ANOTHER PERSON'S character or personality isn't always as simple as it would appear, but can leave the most lasting impression. The key to an effective character compliment is selecting a specific, undeniable quality in the recipient—whether positive or not-so—and casting it in an appealing light. Within this chapter you'll find words of

Death Be Not Disgraced

According to British actor and writer Stephen Fry, many UK newspaper obituaries, in order to not embarrass the memory of the recently deceased, once used code words to describe their subjects' most distasteful qualities. For instance, "a tireless raconteur" was code for "a crashing bore"; describing someone as "convivial" meant they were a drunk; and one who "gave colorful accounts of his exploits" was, in fact, an established liar.

---

reassurance and wisdom that will aid you whenever you're at a loss for the just-right thing to say, as well as comments that may sound positive, but have that all-important subtext of harsh reality.

There's no need to wax overly poetic, but do avoid clichéd turns of phrase in favor of specificity, which will give your compliment the ring of sincerity (e.g., "I love sitting next to you at parties"). Faint praise can also serve as a humorous way to console a friend about an undeniable flaw. This tactic can even provide a humane way to address an otherwise untouchable subject. For example, if a friend is a loutish jerk, you might compliment him for not being afraid to hurt people's feelings. If necessary, you may want to point out the obvious (in pseudo-complimentary form, of course)— e.g., "You certainly aren't afraid of people thinking you're a loutish jerk." Then, if the need arises, it's only a matter of degrees to turn such a kudo into a true backhanded compliment by simply adjusting your tone and facial expression. (You'd be surprised what you can get away with when you smile, though!)

Wit

I'm surprised you haven't cut yourself on your razor sharp wit.

Your quips are the only thing keeping me on Facebook.

You're so funny I almost forget what you look like.

Your foot may always be in your mouth, but you're hilarious!

You're witty enough to make me snort milk out of my nose.

You're such a smart-ass, I'll bet you could sit on a carton of ice cream and tell what flavor it is.

Everybody loves a good pun.

PERSONALITY

You put the wit in witless.

———•———

Your maturity is so inspiring.

———•———

Is it exhausting to be the smartest person in the room?

Charm

You're as smooth as a Zambonied hockey rink.

———•———

You're so charming, even misanthropes like you.

———•———

Bees must love you because you're so sweet.

———•———

Your personality is so magnetic it confuses compasses.

———•———

You could charm the pants off a nun.

You make everything look so easy—
it's like you're not even trying.

You're smoother than butter
on a hot griddle.

What you lack in experience
you make up in charm.

Humility

It's so refreshing to talk
to someone who doesn't feel the
need to prove they are smart.

I feel lucky to be
friends with someone as
self-important as you.

You're so humble. It's almost
like you never won
all those awards you just
told me about.

PERSONALITY

You're not bossy—
you're assertive.

———

You don't get caught up
in shallow pursuits.

———

I wish I could be as
comfortable in my skin
as you are—you seem
very comfortable.

Tip: Try It Open-Faced

The praise sandwich—sandwiching criticism between two layers of praise—is a popular technique thought to soften the sting of negative feedback. But some jaded targets may prefer you get right to the hearty filling, using the criticism to spur themselves to new levels of mastery. More sensitive souls, however, still want a buffer before and after, so try to judge your mark's appetite for straight talk before you offer up any disapproval.

Optimism

You're a big plate of sunshine with a side order of fabulous.

———

No one looks on the bright side as much as you do.

———

Your positive attitude speaks to your charming naiveté.

———

Your optimism in the face of utter failure is inspiring.

Perseverance

You're the tortoise to everyone's hare.

———

You're as persistent as glitter.

———

One day, you'll show them all!

PERSONALITY

I admire someone who won't take "no" for an answer. Or "forget about it," or "cut it out, you ass," or "Stop! This is the police!"

Everyone fails, but it takes a real commitment to do it so spectacularly.

You make the Little Engine that Could look like the Little Engine that Might Have If He Hadn't Been Such a Wimp.

Taste

Your taste is timeless.

You truly know the difference between a house and a home.

Your house looks exactly like the house I wanted when I was eight.

Wax fruit will *never* go out of style!

Don't Worry, Be Happy

When your friends are feeling blue, point them toward a powerful ally of the compliment—positive psychology. A growing body of research indicates that people can boost their sense of well-being by transforming their attitudes about happiness. The approach has gained academic and scientific ground since its introduction in the 1990s: Positive Psychology is one of the most popular courses at Harvard, and similar courses are offered at many American colleges.

You have such a refreshingly ironic approach to decorating.

Taste is something you've clearly acquired—from where, I'm not yet sure.

Honesty

If your honesty were any more refreshing, you could bottle it.

PERSONALITY

When you're as authentic as
you are, not necessarily
everyone will like you.

I know I can always count on you
for the unvarnished truth.

Your honesty would make
Abe Lincoln jealous.

You aren't cynical—you're just a realist.

That wasn't lying. That was
being creative with the facts.

It's not everyone who can live so
comfortably without a conscience.

Eccentricity

You sure march to the beat of
your own drum, don't you?

They may call you wacky,
but never boring.

You were so good at eccentric that
you've graduated to full-on nuts.

You were born in the wrong century.

You really use crazy to your advantage.

With all those enchanting personalities,
you must never be lonely.

Some people may call you OCD, but
you can come clean my house any time.

Likeability

If Oprah knew you, you'd be
one of her favorite things.

You actually make me like myself.

PERSONALITY

You're the kind of catch they need in the majors.

Middle school would have been far less miserable with you there.

Ivory soap is jealous of your purity.

You have the honor of being one of my favorite people.

You're the moment when the ibuprofen kicks in.

Call the police, because your kindness is killing me.

Your prom date still thinks about you.

Do you find it irritating to have those bluebirds and butterflies circling your head all the time?

Loathability

I will always cherish the initial misconceptions I had about you.

You must have been the coolest bully in high school.

Your laugh is infectious, like syphilis.

People may judge you, but they can't argue with your success record.

Your passive aggression really keeps me on my best behavior.

I don't think you're an asshole, but I seem to be in the minority.

If you don't look out for yourself, who will?

PERSONALITY

I wish I could be as ambitious
as you, but I don't like the
squishy sound it makes
when I step on people.

———

I admire the way you
never give away anything that you
can use to your advantage.

———

Nobody's perfect.

The Smiling Town Crier

Social media is challenging the old adage that bad news sells. Disastrous headlines do capture eyeballs, but it's good news that people actually share most. For instance, science articles are more likely to be forwarded because they inspire awe in readers. According to University of Pennsylvania psychologist Jonah Berger, "When you share a story with your friends and peers . . . you don't want them to think of you as a Debbie Downer."

PRIVATE LIFE

When home is where the heart is

WHEN YOU RETREAT FROM THE hubbub of the rat race, you want the course of your home life to run as smoothly as possible. From family to friends, from roomies to potential pickups, the people in your private life have the ability to affect your entire personal paradigm. Employing the flattery in this chapter will artfully maneuver any obstacles

Pickup Artists Take Note

The full 185-word title of the 1658 handbook "The Mysteries of Love & Eloquence, or, the Arts of Wooing and Complementing . . . " touts "Epithets, and flourishing Similitudes, Alphabetically collected, and so properly applied to their several Subjects, that they may be admirably useful . . . " Let's hope "With your Ambrosiack kisses bathe my lips" and "You walk in artificial clouds and bathe your silken limbs in wanton dalliance" work for you, too.

---

out of your way, and may even convince others to do things exactly the way you want them.

After all, home is where the heart is, and you better believe that your loved—and liked—ones hold the key to your well-being in their hands. You know you want to keep *them* happy so you can be happy as well. The very best way to engender those warm-and-fuzzy mutual feelings is a deftly administered daily dose of praise and adulation.

Using the lines in this chapter ensures that the love keeps flowing all the time. As a matter of fact, your existence will soon take on the kind of sunshine-and-rainbows aura that usually only exists in laundry commercials. But don't dismiss the power of the "neg." Maintaining your position in the power plays that occur in all families and many social situations might be your smartest move yet, and delivering an insult that sounds almost like a compliment can keep you at the top of the pack. Moreover, don't we also owe our loved ones the respect shown by our brutal honesty?

Parents

I wouldn't be so perfect if you weren't such brilliant parents.

Would you mind letting someone else have a chance to win Parent of the Year?

You're surprisingly unembarrassing.

Your sanity does a superb job of balancing out Dad's crazy.

All the cool kids wish they had you as parents.

I can't think of a better set of parents to take me on a long, boring vacation.

Your loving dysfunction made me who I am today.

You dress pretty nice for a mom.

You dress pretty cool for a dad.

I always felt like you were there,
even though you never were.

Thanks, Mom and Dad.
Your emotional distance
made me stronger.

Children

Finally, I know what all
those proud parent bumper
stickers are talking about.

You're not half bad, half-pint.

My genes look really good on you.

You're my least disappointing child.

I look back fondly on all your disobedient moments.

Changing your diaper was the highlight of my day.

There will always be a room for you in the basement.

Lugging you around made me the ultimate chick magnet.

Losing my youthful good looks to raise you was totally worth it.

I appreciate the nuance you've found in the word "whatever."

I used to love cleaning your messy little face. I suppose now your wife does, too.

All your needs were special to me.

PRIVATE LIFE

Siblings

Mom always liked you best.

You always deserved
the top bunk.

There is no one in
my life as fun, as loving,
or as irritating as you.

Great Job!

Parents: enough with the compliments! According to researchers, kids who are told they're great all the time can't cope when they inevitably fail at something. Children lauded for efforts, rather than characteristics, are more resilient and more willing to challenge themselves. The theory: if you praise kids for their effort, they're likely to connect their self-worth to their attempts rather than their successes.

If you got the brains and the body, what did I get?

Ours isn't a sibling rivalry—it's a sibling lovelry.

We're like the Brady Bunch, but without all that smiling.

Congrats! You still act like the youngest and look like the oldest.

You should consider it a compliment that you can still make me mad.

I would have made a great only child.

Relatives

Norman Rockwell's got nothing on us.

You guys give in-laws a good name.

I'm so relieved that
our family's crazy
doesn't extend to you.

Thanks for making me look
forward to holidays.

We take family ties to a whole
new level of bondage.

Now I know why the Mafia
calls itself a family.

Mates

Not everyone gets to wake up
next to a work of art.

You are my rose-colored glasses.

You bring home the bacon
and a side of pancakes.

Tip: Avoid the Half-Compliment

According to *Glamour* magazine, going out of your way to avoid sounding as though you're flattering a woman can be almost as bad as openly insulting her. For instance, telling a potential date, "I'm not looking for a supermodel," or "I don't care that much about beauty," might be intended to make you sound down-to-earth. Instead, all it does is tell her that she's average. So take a hint, and go with the sincere compliment.

Our pairing is the greatest since wine met food.

You must be a saint to have stayed married to me for this long.

You complete me, as in completely crazy.

I'm far less pathological with you by my side.

If I didn't have you, I'd never
know when I was wrong!

You fake it so well, I've come
to love all your lies.

Doves mate for life, too—
all their brief, worm-eating lives.

Lovers

I finally get all those Meg Ryan movies.

If they filmed our story, it would be
the perfect balance of rom and com.

We don't just make love—we carefully
construct it plank by plank in the
manner of an Amish barn raising.

Our one-night stand is turning
out to have a bit more longevity.

I'd break a sweat for you.

Before you, I'd never
wanted anyone to talk to me
for hours like that.

Don't worry, babe. I know
how beautiful you can be
when you finally get ready.

You're still the one I'd drunkenly
pick up in a dive bar.

Remember that first time
we met? I'll never look at cheap
motels the same way again.

You weren't easy—I prefer to
think of you as less difficult.

Having nothing interesting to say
makes you such a great listener.

I can't imagine anyone I'd
rather settle for.

Potential Pickups & One-Night Stands

If you were any hotter, you'd
come with a warning label.

Can anyone look you in the
eye with that rack?

It isn't all the drugs—it's you
I'm dazzled by.

I'm hopelessly drawn to you like
a douchebag to a disco ball.

You're the only hot mess I'm
paying attention to tonight.

You're even better
in the sack than I am!

You turn ordinary hanky-panky
into full on freaky-deaky.

Sex with you is the next
best thing to sex alone.

You must get all the hotties
with low self-esteem.

If you're going to regret this in the
morning, we can sleep past noon.

I think I've fallen in hate with you.

As soon as you said "hey,"
we were rolling in it.

Friends & Frenemies

You're the person I'd want with
me if I were homesteading on
the prairie in a sod house.

PRIVATE LIFE

You are my Ethel Mertz.

———

You make it hard to
be a misanthrope.

———

You keep my ego from
getting out of control.

———

Thanks for making me a
Bert to your Ernie.

Private Affairs

Sometimes, it doesn't matter what you say, only when and where you say it. One unfortunate hotel worker says he was fired from his job when he told one hotel visitor how another guest, the actress Jennifer Aniston, was "very sweet and much more petite than I thought." It seems even this polite compliment violated the hotel's strict privacy policy—proof that knowing when to speak and when to be discreet is key.

I'm jealous of all your close friends.

You've ruined my streak of
hating everyone I meet.

You give the best bad relationship advice.

You're smart to do your
laundry on Saturday night,
when everyone else is out.

If we crashed in the Andes,
I would eat you last.

Hanging out with you is a
great warm-up for spending the
day with my idiotic boss.

Roomies & Neighbors

With a roomie like you, why would
anyone ever want to live alone?

I love the obsessive-compulsive
cleanliness part of your mental disorder.

Thanks for showing me how good
all my clothes look on you.

Congrats on breaking
your own record for the tallest
pile of dirty dishes.

Living with you is like living with
a cleaner version of a neat freak.

Having you as a roomie
makes me love very large
rooms even more.

Overhearing your loud sex helps
keep my porn costs low.

Your tall fence makes you
a good neighbor.

PUBLIC LIFE
When you're out and about

THE WORLD CAN BE A HARSH and lonely place. People rushing about, doing their daily chores, going to work, dealing with authority—who has the time or the energy to be nice? But it can pay off to make the effort. Sailing breezily through life requires more than a platinum credit card and ample confidence. You must get people on your side, which happens more easily and

Well Played

Artful workplace flattery can take you far if you can simultaneously compliment your boss and prove you've been paying attention. When you comment on an exec's presentation, advises etiquette maven Marjabelle Young Stewart, keep it concise and mention specific points that caught your attention. Odds are, according to flattery expert Richard Stengel, your boss won't see your words as empty praise, just excellent judgment.

---

elegantly with a good word than with a smile or even a cash tip.

What really opens doors, allows you to avoid trouble, or gets you that extra shot of espresso in your half-caf latte? The well-timed delivery of a comment chosen from this chapter can ease your way through the treacherous landscape of the world at large. The old adage "You can catch more flies with honey than with vinegar" is a cliché, true, but it's a cliché *because* it's true. Of course, don't feel pressured to sugarcoat reality if you have a valid observation that's a little less than laudatory.

Speaking of being out in the world, why does mixing business with pleasure get such a bad rap? Perhaps nowhere is the fine art of asskissery more important than in the workplace. At times you may need to sincerely curry favor with the powers that be, while at other times you may want to cultivate allies among your coworkers. And don't forget, the backhanded compliment often shines its brightest on the job, where you can keep people occupied as they busily interpret the mixed signals you choose to send out.

At the Store

You're the first customer today
that I didn't want to kill.

I bet you're always right, even
when you're not a customer.

It's been a pleasure taking
orders from you.

You're the type of customer that
makes me love coming to work.

You really put the service
in customer service.

Somehow you've turned
condescension into an art form.

The way you follow me around
the store makes me feel so safe.

On the Go

I'd bring contraband to
this airport just for the pleasure
of having you frisk me.

I didn't know TSA stood for
tall, sexy, and awesome.

I feel so much safer knowing you're
the one looking through my suitcase.

You work that wand better
than Harry Potter.

When our flight ends, can
I take you home with me?

You push that cart with such precision.

Clearly you are the in-flight
entertainment.

On the Town

Forget the drinks—you should charge for your advice.

———•———

You're strictly top-shelf.

———•———

If you keep serving me, my relationship will be what's on the rocks.

———•———

With you around, I don't need any sugar in my coffee.

———•———

You are the Van Gogh of cappuccino-foam artists.

———•———

I don't take pictures of just any latte, you know.

———•———

Wow, you actually make that look difficult.

PUBLIC LIFE

The menu looks good. It would
look better if you were on it.

I like a waiter who is not afraid to fawn.

Even Gunga Din couldn't bring
water to the table faster than you.

You make it worth eating
the crappy food here.

Don't Be Rude, Dude

According to a 2008 University of Florida study, rudeness impacts problem-solving and creativity skills, even when the rudeness is merely imagined. That diminished productivity can also directly affect the bottom line. According to a Georgetown professor's 2011 study, workers will avoid coworkers—or even work—just to dodge more rudeness. The bottom line? The bottom line is positively affected when negativity is banished.

Under the Weather

With a doctor like you, I wish
I could be sick all the time.

———•———

You could make someone look
forward to a colonoscopy.

———•———

You warmed the speculum to
just the right temperature.

———•———

Your bedside manner
perfectly suits the sterile,
stainless steel bed that
graces your office.

———•———

If there's anyone I would
ever want to have his
hands in my mouth for
an hour, it's you.

———•———

You make my child scream
less than any other nurse.

PUBLIC LIFE

I love the way you say,
"This is going to sting a little."

I bet all the pharmaceutical
reps try to get your number.

Do you ever miss worrying
about your own problems?

It's too bad you'll never know how
much you've really helped me.

You make me as relaxed as
a frog in a gently
warming pot of water.

In Custody

That gown really brings out
your eyes, Your Honor.

You're such a great judge—of character.

Tip: Bring an Apple

Brownnosing might give you a bad name, but it turns out a little posterior smooching goes a long way in the job market. Studies show, complimenting your interviewer's appearance and agreeing with their opinions beat touting your own abilities in landing that job. In fact, social attraction, or the "similar-to-me bias," is rated second only to appearance in interpersonal attraction. So, polish those shoes *and* that apple and go get 'em, tiger.

You make me want to lawyer up.

———

All that ambulance chasing has given you great legs.

———

You're so considerate, Officer. I've never been arrested this well before.

———

You have an eye for the subtler parking violations.

PUBLIC LIFE

Cuffs. Mirrored shades. Pistol cocked.
You're like Tom of Finland's wet dream.

———•——

I'm not drunk. You just look so sexy
in your uniform that I've forgotten
my name, and the alphabet, and
how to walk in a straight line.

———•——

I'm not sure which is brighter, the
flashing lights or your smile.

———•——

I feel so much safer knowing that
you're protecting our community
from dangerous jaywalkers.

In Class

You make me dream of Latin declensions.

———•——

You put the dish in petri dish.

———•——

You've taught me things no book could.

You're by far my favorite subject.

I'd like to instantiate your objects,
and access their member variables.

I fell asleep because your lecture
was so peaceful and comforting.

Hey, you're the big fish—in a small pond.

That's a particularly vibrant shade of
red ink you used all over my paper.

At the Office

I've always wanted to work for the best.

I knew you were a genius
when you hired me.

If you moved my cheese, I'd
enjoy looking for it.

PUBLIC LIFE

You're not bossy—you're totally boss.

I should be giving you a raise.

You could make a spreadsheet exciting.

I can't imagine being micro-managed by anyone else.

You put the Power in PowerPoint.

You inspire us all
to desperately please you.

My ideas always sound so much
better coming from you.

Pretty soon I'll be reporting to you.

You look so much better than
your LinkedIn profile picture.

I can't think of anyone who deserved
my promotion more than you.

It's quite masterful, the way
you ream out the staff.

Your leadership has inspired
me to resent my paycheck
withholdings slightly less.

No one knows how to rock
an invoice quite like you.

You could really hurt someone
with all that follow-through.

I love what you've done with
your half-cubicle.

You are the King Pimp of paper pushers.

You're the e.e. cummings of email.

PUBLIC LIFE

You probably didn't even have to sleep with anyone to get this job.

Your photocopying skills make you stand out here greatly.

For a surly, hostile receptionist, you're actually quite helpful.

This is so impressive . . . for you.

Tip: Pay a Compliment

In the service industry world, it's known as "the verbal tip"—giving effusive praise instead of cash—and it's rarely welcome. However, researchers have shown flattery lights up the same portion of the brain as cash. They also found praise improved learning over time. Can you imagine how customer service would improve if you coupled a generous gratuity with some nongratuitous compliments?

FAMOUS FLATTERY

When notoriety is noticed

CONSIDER CYRANO DE BERGERAC: this fictional French wordsmith wrote magnificent love poems, then allowed his friend to take all the credit for them. Wouldn't it be grand if you had your own Cyrano to compose some exalted phrases for you to deliver? How about if some of the finest and wittiest (or at least most honest) minds on earth let you reuse their greatest hits?

Love Notes

From the lute to the Stratocaster, a love song penned for a particular paramour may be the compliment's zenith: witness Eric Clapton's "Layla," Stephen Stills' "Suite: Judy Blue Eyes," or Elvis Costello's "Alison." Of course, a song can also bite—in Carly Simon's classic "You're So Vain," she gleefully mocks a former lover (whose name she still refuses to reveal to the world). You be the judge if an ironic ode is more memorable than a sincere one.

We are all familiar with the mutual admiration society that exists in Hollywood as well as in literary and artistic circles, and *quid pro quo* may as well be printed on the door of every politician's office. Some of our most well-known cultural icons are keenly aware that mutual back-scratching is the best plan for a peaceful coexistence. So look no further than this chapter, where the laudatory paeans of the best and the brightest are on display to choose from whenever you feel in need of that little extra punch.

And speaking of pugilism, the gloves come off from time to time when the glitterati let loose with some mighty one-two jabs. Free-ranging celebrities—absent the impediments of managers and public relations handlers—often deliver well-intentioned but ultimately all-too-revealing comments. Let your own inner pussycat extend its claws with these bitchy and backhanded comments that you can adapt to fit your circumstances.

Passionate Praise

"I want to thank you for working on our marriage for ten Christmases. It's good. It is work, but it's the best kind of work. And there's no one I'd rather work with." —Ben Affleck, to wife Jennifer Garner, *85th Annual Academy Awards*

"Dearest, I think you're the lowest thing that ever crawled, but as long as I can put my hands on you, no other man will ever touch me." —Bette Davis, as Joyce Arden in *It's Love I'm After*

"Everything wrong with you, I like." —Van Johnson, as Ted Randall in *A Guy Named Joe*

"He's got a real pretty mouth, ain't he?" —Herbert "Cowboy" Coward, as Toothless Man in *Deliverance*

"Michael, you are quite the cupid. You can stick an arrow into my buttocks anytime."
—David Cross, as Tobias Fünke in *Arrested Development*

Comedic Commendations

"It's quite possible that no one in history has gotten more laughs than Bob Hope. Why, even his pauses are funnier than most people's punch lines." —Kirk Douglas

---

"Milton Berle recently authored a new book—it's called *Milton Berle: An Autobiography*. I must say I read his book from cover to cover. Luckily I didn't read what's inside." —Dean Martin

---

"I see the great Carl Reiner is here. This is so cool, man. Carl, seriously, congrats on being on color TV for the first time." —Jeffrey Ross, *Comedy Central Roast of Joan Rivers*

"Our next two presenters have done for fake news what the Fox News Channel has done for fake news—please welcome Stephen Colbert and Jon Stewart." —Conan O'Brien, *58th Primetime Emmy Awards*

Acting Accolades

"Meryl Streep holds the record for most nominations as an actress, or as I like to think of it, most losses." —Steve Martin, *82nd Annual Academy Awards*

"He's been nominated for an Emmy three times for his role as hetero hound Barney Stinson on *How I Met Your Mother* not because he's playing straight but because he's very funny. The public's perception of gay men is shifting because of this guy, and they'll be too entertained to notice. That's more than a good trick. That's magic." —Joss Whedon, on Neil Patrick Harris

FAMOUS FLATTERY

"Her fame was greater than her contributions as an actress."
—The *New York Times*, on the death of Marilyn Monroe

"Whatever you do, don't miss *Liz & Dick*. It's an instant classic of unintentional hilarity. Drinking games were made for movies like this." —Tim Goodman, in *The Hollywood Reporter*

Vegan Vanity

Want a little affirmation with your quinoa? California's Café Gratitude offers vegan dishes with a heaping side of sweetness and light. Order "I AM MAGICAL" (veggie burger) or "I AM DAZZLING" (Caesar salad). Your server will reiterate the compliment when you get your food. It's wildly popular with entertainment folks—and since negativity and irony are frowned upon, what better place to go after a bad review?

Filmic Flattery

"Stanley Kubrick and Richard Lester are the only ones that appeal to me—except for the old masters. By which I mean John Ford, John Ford, and John Ford." —Orson Welles

---

"I might as well come out and say that *Transformers: Dark of the Moon* is among Mr. Bay's best movies and by far the best 3-D sequel ever made about gigantic toys from outer space." —*New York Times* film critic A. O. Scott

---

"There really is no point to seeing *Playing for Keeps* unless you would like to have sex with Gerard Butler, or would like to be Gerard Butler, or think, at least, that life inside his shoes would be interesting." —*San Francisco Chronicle* film critic Mick LaSalle

Tuneful Tributes

"What I believe is this: I believe that Bob Dylan and James Brown had a baby. And they abandoned this child on the side of the road, between the exit interchanges of 8A and 9 on the New Jersey Turnpike. That child is Bruce Springsteen." —Jon Stewart

---

"I certainly think she references me a lot in her work. Sometimes I think it's amusing and flattering and well done. I can't really be annoyed by it or insulted by it, because, obviously, I've influenced her." —Madonna, on Lady Gaga

---

"Britney's a very beautiful human being. After I worked with her, I realized that there was a reason why she was the most popular pop artist over so many other pop artists at that time who were more talented, had better voices. And it was because of her heart, her soul."
—Zoe Saldana, on Britney Spears

Business Casual

President Obama found out that personal remarks, even positive ones, can be unwelcome in the workplace when he was publicly vilified for describing California Attorney General Kamala Harris as "by far, the best-looking attorney general." Suddenly the fact that he had also called her brilliant, dedicated, and tough was lost in the uproar. So make sure your choose your praise wisely, and stick to the office-appropriate choices in this book.

Artistic Acclaim

"Yo-Yo Ma . . . has done everything you could do with the cello except climb inside and ride it over Niagara Falls. But you know, you know in your heart that if he ever did, it would totally redefine our preconceived notions of what it can sound like to plunge to your death in a cello." —Stephen Colbert

"Very colourful." —Queen Elizabeth II, on Sir Paul McCartney's paintings

"They are truly shiny." —John Updike, on the work of sculptor Jeff Koons

"The late paintings [by Andy Warhol] are really much better than people think they are." —Art critic Jerry Saltz

Literary Laudations

"At certain points, reading the work can even be said to resemble the act of making love to a three-hundred-pound woman. Once she gets on top, it's over. Fall in love, or be asphyxiated. So you read and you grab and you even find delight in some of these mounds of material. Yet all the while you resist—how you resist!—letting three hundred pounds take you over." —Norman Mailer, on Tom Wolfe's *A Man in Full*

"Anyone who lives to read gorgeous writing will want to lick this book and sleep with it between their legs."
—Dave Eggers, on Daniel Handler's *Adverbs*

"[F. Scott Fitzgerald] had one of the rarest qualities in all literature . . . one is almost ashamed to use it to describe a real distinction. Nevertheless, the word is charm—charm as Keats would have used it . . . It's not a matter of pretty writing or clear style. It's a kind of subdued magic, controlled and exquisite, the sort of thing you get from good string quartets." —Raymond Chandler

---

"[*Lord of the Flies*] . . . was, so far as I can remember, the first book with hands—strong ones that reached out of the pages and seized me by the throat. It said to me, 'This is not just entertainment; it's life-or-death.'"
—Stephen King, on William Golding

"At his best Crichton is a blend of Stephen Jay Gould and Agatha Christie . . . Animals—especially, if not quite exclusively, velociraptors—are what he's good at. People are what he is bad at. People, and prose." —Martin Amis, on Michael Crichton's *The Lost World*

Beauty Blandishments

"Mel Gibson is somewhere to the right of Attila the Hun. He's beautiful, but only on the outside." —Susan Sarandon

"Helen Gurley Brown, who as the author of *Sex and the Single Girl* shocked early-1960s America with the news that unmarried women not only had sex but thoroughly enjoyed it . . . died on Monday in Manhattan. She was 90, though parts of her were considerably younger." —Margalit Fox, in an obituary for the *New York Times*

"Your husband had told me you were the most beautiful woman he'd ever met. I didn't expect the most beautiful woman that *I'd* ever met." —George Clooney, as Miles Massey in *Intolerable Cruelty*

"Madonna has done so much, and she's been around so long, and the bitch still looks good!" —Britney Spears

---

"I mean, I wish I could've gained twenty pounds and played Effie." —Beyoncé, on Jennifer Hudson's Oscar buzz (and later win) for the movie *Dreamgirls*

Personality Paeans

"I want to take this opportunity to say how proud I am of my little brother— my dear, sweet, talented brother. Just imagine what you could accomplish if you tried celibacy!" —Shirley MacLaine, on Warren Beatty

FAMOUS FLATTERY

"People often come up and say what a thrill it must be to be asked to play a role in a Clint Eastwood movie and it is, breathtakingly so. You read the script, you wait, the telephone rings, it's Clint on the line. He asks, 'Will you play the role for one hundred thousand dollars?' With great excitement you say, 'Yes, Clint, absolutely. Can you give me three days to raise the hundred thousand dollars?'" —Donald Sutherland

King of Praise

In publishing, a quick path to getting noticed might be a back-cover blurb from author Gary Shteyngart, the man *Time* magazine calls "the reigning blurb king." Shteyngart's "promiscuous praise" has decorated the covers of over a hundred books. "I look for the following," Shteyngart explained of his motivation: "two covers, one spine, at least 40 pages, ISBN number, title, author's name. Once those conditions are satisfied, I blurb. And I blurb hard."

"This bloviating ignoramus . . . Donald Trump is redundant evidence that if your net worth is high enough, your IQ can be very low and you can still intrude into American politics." —George Will

---

"What can I say about our next two presenters? The first is an actor, producer, writer, and director whose movies have grossed over three and a half billion dollars at the box office. He's won two Academy Awards and three Golden Globes for his powerful and varied, performances starring in such films as *Philadelphia*, *Forrest Gump*, *Cast Away*, *Apollo 13*, and *Saving Private Ryan*. The other . . . is Tim Allen." —Ricky Gervais, *68th Annual Golden Globe Awards*

Tom Hanks: "Like many of you, we recall back when Ricky Gervais was a slightly chubby but very kind comedian."
Tim Allen: "Neither of which is he now."
—*68th Annual Golden Globe Awards*

Political Puffery

"I think that what people are responding to is that great sort of vitality, confidence. It doesn't matter that the confidence is based on a kind of total ignorance. It's a vitality about her that people like, an unequivocal, in the present, raw, visceral quality that she has." —Tina Brown, on Sarah Palin

---

"I believe that Ronald Reagan can make this country what it once was . . . an arctic region covered with ice." —Steve Martin

---

"[Jimmy] Carter is a far better ex-president than he was a president." —Hendrik Hertzberg

---

"Bill Clinton's virtues and his flaws are so exaggerated and so public that we see ourselves in him." —Michael Takiff, in *The Huffington Post*

"I can't imagine being micromanaged by anyone else."